What Is the International Monetary Fund?

by David D. Driscoll

External Relations Department
International Monetary Fund
Washington, D.C.

ISBN: 1-55775-408-x

Revised July 1997

To order additional copies of this publication or a
catalog of other IMF publications, please contact:

International Monetary Fund, Publication Services
700 19th Street, N.W., Washington, D.C. 20431, U.S.A.
Tel.: (202) 623-7430   Telefax: (202) 623-7201
E-mail: publications@imf.org
Internet: http://www.imf.org

What Is the International Monetary Fund?

*e*xcept to a small circle of economists and financial officials, the International Monetary Fund is a mysterious presence on the international scene. Considerable confusion reigns about why it exists and what it does. Some observers, confusing it with the World Bank or another aid institution, are under the impression that the IMF exists to subsidize economic development in the poorer nations. Others imagine it as an international central bank controlling the creation of money on a world scale. Still others regard the IMF as a powerful and disapproving political institution, imbued with a missionary zeal for fiscal rectitude, that somehow compels its members to tread a path of economic austerity. The IMF is in fact none of these. It is neither a development bank, nor a world central bank, nor an agency that can or wishes to coerce its members to do very much of anything. It is rather a cooperative institution that 181 countries have voluntarily joined because they see the advantage of consulting with one another in this forum to maintain a stable system of buying and selling their currencies so that payments in foreign money can take place between countries smoothly and without delay. The Fund is the enemy of surprise. Members of the IMF believe that keeping other countries informed of their intentions regarding policies that influence payments by the government and private residents of one country to those of another, rather than making a secret of such policies, is to everyone's advantage. They also believe that occasionally modifying those policies (by devaluing the currency, for instance), when fellow members agree that this is in the common interest, will help international trade to grow and will create more and higher-paying jobs in an expanding world economy. The IMF lends money to members having trouble meeting financial obligations to other members, but only on condition that they under-

*"Widespread convert-
ibility now permits easy
exchange between most
of the world's major
currencies."*

take economic reforms to
eliminate these difficulties for
their own good and that of
the entire membership.

Contrary to widespread per-
ception, the IMF has no
effective authority over the domestic economic policies of its
members. It is in no position, for example, to force a member to
spend more on schools or hospitals and less on buying military
aircraft or constructing grandiose presidential palaces. It can, and
often does, urge members to make the best use of scarce resources by refraining from senseless military expenditures or by
spending more money on the environment. Unfortunately, members can, and often do, ignore this well-intentioned advice. In this
case, the IMF can only try, through rational argument, to per-
suade such a member of the domestic and international benefits
of adopting policies favored by the membership as a whole. There
is no question of forcing a member to adopt any policy. What authority the IMF does possess is confined to requiring the member
to disclose information on its monetary and fiscal policies and to
avoid, as far as possible, putting restrictions on exchanging domestic for foreign currency and on making payments to other
members.

Its members have given the IMF some authority over their payments policies because these policies are of paramount impor-
tance to the flow of money between nations and because
experience has confirmed that without a global monitoring
agency the modern system of payments in foreign currency simply
does not work. Changing money is the central point of financial
contact between nations and the indispensable vehicle of world
trade. Each currency, be it the dollar, franc, or something more
exotic like the Gambian dalasi or Haitian gourde, has a value in
terms of other currencies. The relative or exchange value of the
world's major currencies now fluctuates continuously, to the de-
light or misery of currency traders, and is reported daily in the
financial columns of the newspapers. Although the operations of

the exchange market, where money (much the same as such commodities as wheat or apples) is bought and sold, may seem remote from daily life, these operations profoundly affect us all. Most commonly, we experience the reality of exchange values abruptly when we travel abroad as tourists and find we must first buy local money before we can buy anything else. Purchasing foreign currency is a fact of life not only for tourists, but also for importers, banks, governments, and other institutions that must acquire foreign currency, often on a very large scale, before they can do business abroad.

Take, for example, a bicycle importer in Copenhagen who tries to buy from a dealer in Tokyo 100 Japanese bicycles for sale at 30,000 yen each. The Japanese dealer will not accept payment in Danish kroner, for which he has no immediate use: he cannot pay his suppliers or employees in kroner or even buy his lunch at the local noodle shop using Danish money. He wants yen. The Danish importer must therefore have enough kroner converted to make up the 3 million yen for the shipment. It is not difficult to change kroner into yen (any bank in Copenhagen will be happy to do so), because both the Danish and Japanese governments are committed to the convertibility of their respective currencies. Neither country restricts the exchange of its national currency into another national money, and this greatly facilitates international trade.

Fortunately, widespread convertibility now permits easy exchange between most of the world's major currencies. Convertibility has allowed virtually unrestricted travel, trade, and investment during the past quarter of a century and has resulted largely from the cooperation of member nations with the IMF in eliminating restrictions on buying and selling national currencies.

The present confident expectation that one currency will be converted into another on demand makes it difficult to imagine circumstances in which this was not the case. And yet it was largely in reaction to circumstances of widespread inconvertibility and related exchange problems that the international community decided over 50 years ago to work out these problems in a common forum that was to become the International Monetary Fund.

Origins

The need for an organization like the IMF became evident during the Great Depression that ravaged the world economy in the 1930s. Most of us are familiar with that era through dramatic photographs of farms eroding away in duststorms and of lines of jobless men waiting to enter soup kitchens. The Depression was devastating to all forms of economic life. Banks failed by the thousands, leaving bewildered depositors penniless, agricultural prices fell below the cost of production, land values plummeted, abandoned farms reverted to wilderness, factories stood idle, fleets waited in harbors for cargoes that never materialized, and tens of millions of workers walked the streets in search of jobs that did not exist.

The devastation was not confined to the visible economy. It was no less destructive of the unseen world of international finance and monetary exchange. A widespread lack of confidence in paper money led to a demand for gold beyond what national treasuries could supply. A number of nations, led by the United Kingdom, were consequently forced to abandon the gold standard, which, by defining the value of each currency in terms of a given amount of gold, had for years given money a known and stable value. Because of uncertainty about the value of money that no longer bore a fixed relation to gold, exchanging money became very difficult between those nations that remained on the gold standard and those that did not. Nations hoarded gold and money that could be converted into gold, further contracting the amount and frequency of monetary transactions between nations, eliminating jobs, and lowering living standards. Moreover, some governments severely restricted the exchange of domestic for foreign money and even searched for barter schemes (for example, a locomotive for 100 tons of coffee) that would eliminate the use of money completely. Other governments, desperate to find foreign buyers for domestic agricultural products, made these products appear cheaper by selling their national money below its real value so as to undercut the trade of other nations selling the same products. This practice, known as competitive devaluation, merely

Growth in IMF Membership, 1994–97

(Number of countries)

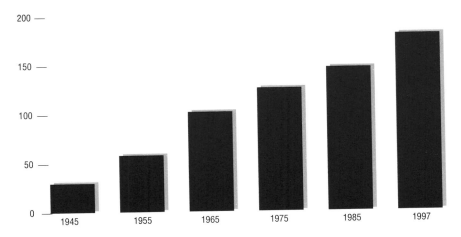

evoked retaliation through similar devaluation by trading rivals. The relation between money and the value of goods became confused, as did the relation between the value of one national currency and another. Under these conditions the world economy languished. Between 1929 and 1932 prices of goods fell by 48 percent worldwide, and the value of international trade fell by 63 percent.

Several international conferences convened during the 1930s to address world monetary problems ended in failure. Partial and tentative solutions were clearly inadequate. What was required was cooperation on a previously untried scale by all nations in establishing an innovative monetary system and an international institution to monitor it. Fortunately, in a happy coincidence, two bold and original thinkers, Harry Dexter White in the United States and John Maynard Keynes in the United Kingdom, put forward almost simultaneously in the early 1940s proposals for just such a system, to be supervised not by occasional international meetings

5

but by a permanent cooperative organization. The system, reacting to the needs of the times, would encourage the unrestricted conversion of one currency into another, establish a clear and unequivocal value for each currency, and eliminate restrictions and practices, such as competitive devaluations, that had brought investment and trade to a virtual standstill during the 1930s. After much negotiation under difficult wartime conditions, the international community accepted the system and an organization to supervise it. Final negotiations for establishing the International Monetary Fund took place among the delegates of 44 nations gathered at Bretton Woods, New Hampshire, U.S.A. in July 1944. The IMF began operations in Washington, D.C. in May 1946. It then had 39 members.

The IMF's membership now numbers 181 countries. Membership is open to every country that conducts its own foreign policy and is willing to adhere to the IMF charter of rights and obligations. All major countries are now members of the IMF. The formerly centrally planned economies of Eastern Europe and the former Soviet Union have become members and are well on their way to becoming market economies. Members can leave the IMF whenever they wish. Cuba, Czechoslovakia (now the Czech Republic and Slovak Republic), Indonesia, and Poland have in fact done so in the past, although all these countries, with the exception of Cuba, subsequently reconsidered their decisions and eventually rejoined the institution.

Quotas and Voting

On joining the IMF, each member country contributes a certain sum of money called a quota subscription, as a sort of membership fee.

Quotas serve various purposes. First, they form a pool of money that the IMF can draw from to lend to members in financial difficulty. Second, they are the basis for determining how much the contributing member can borrow from the IMF or receives from the IMF in periodic allocations of special assets known as SDRs (special drawing rights). The more a member contributes, the

Largest IMF Members, by Quota, 1997

(In millions of SDRs and percent of total quotas)

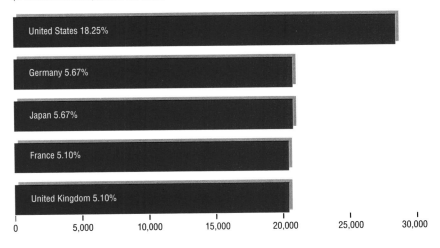

United States 18.25%

Germany 5.67%

Japan 5.67%

France 5.10%

United Kingdom 5.10%

0   5,000   10,000   15,000   20,000   25,000   30,000

more it can borrow in time of need. Third, they determine the voting power of the member. The IMF itself, through an analysis of each country's wealth and economic performance, sets the amount of the quota the member will contribute. The richer the country, the higher its quota. Quotas are reviewed every five years and can be raised or lowered according to the needs of the IMF and the economic prosperity of the member. In 1945, the then 35 members of the IMF paid in $7.6 billion; by 1997, IMF members had paid in more than $200 billion. The United States, with the world's largest economy, contributes most to the IMF, providing about 18 percent of total quotas (around $38 billion); the Marshall Islands, an island republic in the Pacific, has the smallest quota, contributing about $3.6 million.

The founding nations reasoned in 1944 that the IMF would function most efficiently and decisions would be made most responsibly by relating members' voting power directly to the

7

amount of money they contribute to the institution through their quotas. Those who contribute most to the IMF are therefore given the strongest voice in determining its policies. Thus, the United States now has about 265,000 votes, or about 18 percent of the total; the Marshall Islands has 275.

Organization

Many people view the IMF as an institution of great authority and independence and assume that it decides the best economic policies for its members to pursue, dictates these decisions to the membership, and then makes sure its members conform. Nothing could be further from the truth. Far from being dictated to by the IMF, the membership itself dictates to the IMF the policies it will follow. The chain of command runs clearly from the governments of member countries to the IMF and not vice versa. In setting out the obligations of individual members to the IMF, or in working out details of loan agreements with a member, the IMF acts not on its own but as an intermediary between the will of the majority of the membership and the individual member country.

The top link of the chain of command is the Board of Governors, one from each member, and an equal number of Alternate Governors. As the Governors and their Alternates are ministers of finance or heads of central banks, they speak authoritatively for their governments. The oddly named Interim Committee (it has existed since the 1970s) gives them advice on the functioning of the international monetary system, and a joint IMF/World Bank Development Committee advises them on the special needs of poorer countries. Since Governors and Alternates are fully occupied in their own capitals, they gather only on the occasion of annual meetings to deal formally and as a group with IMF matters.

During the rest of the year, the Governors communicate the wishes of their governments for the IMF's day-to-day work to their representatives who form the IMF's Executive Board at headquarters in Washington. The 24 Executive Directors, meeting at least three times a week in formal session, supervise the implementation of policies set by member governments through the Board of Governors. At present, eight Executive Directors represent individual countries: China, France, Germany, Japan, Russia, Saudi Arabia, the United Kingdom, and the United States. Sixteen other Executive Directors each represent groupings of the remaining countries. The Executive Board rarely makes its decisions on the basis of formal voting, but relies on the formation of consensus among its members, a practice that minimizes confrontation on sensitive issues and promotes agreement on the decisions ultimately taken.

"The chain of command runs clearly from the governments of member countries to the IMF and not vice versa."

The IMF has a staff of about 2,200, headed by a Managing Director, who is also chairman of the Executive Board, which appoints him. By tradition, the Managing Director is a European, or at least a non-American. (The President of the World Bank is traditionally a U.S. national.) The international staff comes from 121 countries and comprises mainly economists, but also statisticians, research scholars, experts in public finance and taxation, linguists, writers, and support personnel. Most staff members work at IMF headquarters in Washington, though a few are assigned to small offices in Paris, Geneva, Tokyo, and at the United Nations in New York, or represent the IMF on temporary assignment in member countries. Unlike Executive Directors, who represent specific countries, staff members are international civil servants; they are responsible to the membership as a whole in carrying out IMF policies and do not represent national interests.

Operations

On joining the IMF, a member country undertakes to keep other members informed about its arrangements for determining the value of its money in relation to the money of other countries, to refrain from restricting the exchange of its money for foreign money, and to pursue economic policies that will increase in an orderly and constructive way its own national wealth and that of the whole membership. Members obligate themselves to follow

9

this code of conduct. As noted above, the IMF has no means of co-ercing them to live up to these obligations, although it can and does exert moral pressure to encourage them to conform to the rules and regulations they have freely agreed to observe. If a country persistently ignores its obligations, the rest of the membership working through the IMF may declare the offending member ineligible to borrow money or, as a last resort, can ask the member to resign from the institution. Normally, however, it is taken for granted that the member wishes to cooperate as far as it can with the general aims of the IMF (otherwise it would not have bothered to join), and that any lapse in fulfilling the self-imposed obligations of membership is a result of factors beyond the member's immediate control.

Over the years the membership has assigned to the IMF a variety of duties appropriate to the changing needs of the times, and the IMF has proven remarkably flexible in carrying out these duties. At present, the membership has charged the IMF with the responsibility of supervising a cooperative system for the orderly exchange of national currencies, lending money to members to reorganize their economies so as to cooperate better within the system, and providing auxiliary services—including technical assistance—to assist members in implementing policies beneficial to the whole membership.

Exchange Arrangements

In its early years, all members joining the IMF undertook to follow the same method of calculating the exchange value of their money. They did so according to what was called the par (equal) value system. In those days, the United States defined the value of its dollar in terms of gold, so that one ounce of gold was equal to exactly $35. The U.S. government stood behind this definition and would exchange gold for dollars at that rate on demand. On joining the IMF, all other members had to define the exchange value of their money in terms of gold as well, and since two things equal to a third are equal to each other, the value of each currency was, for the sake of convenience, commonly quoted in terms of the U.S. dollar. Members kept the value of their money within 1 percent of this par value, and if they felt a change would help their economy, they discussed the contemplated change with other members in the forum of the IMF and obtained their consent before implementing it. The par value system had the wonderful advantage of keeping currencies stable and predictable, a great help to international investors, traders, and travelers, but over the years it also developed a number of disadvantages. It was a wrenching experience, attended by great political risk, for a government to change the par value of its currency, and each change in the par value of a major currency tended to become a crisis for the whole system. The par value system served the world well for about 25 years. It came to an end in the early 1970s, however, when U.S. gold reserves proved inadequate to meet the demand for gold in exchange for the dollars presented by those who regarded gold at $35 an ounce an irresistible bargain.

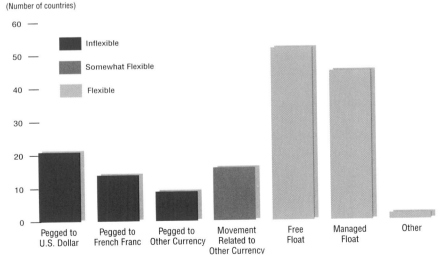

How Members Determine Exchange Values
(Number of countries)

Inflexible

Somewhat Flexible

Flexible

Pegged to U.S. Dollar | Pegged to French Franc | Pegged to Other Currency | Movement Related to Other Currency | Free Float | Managed Float | Other

Since the abandonment of the par value system, the membership of the IMF has agreed to allow each member to choose its own method of determining the exchange value of its money. The only requirements are that the member no longer base the value of its currency on gold and inform other members about precisely how it is determining the currency's value. The choice is wide. Many large industrial nations allow their currencies to float freely: their money is worth whatever the markets are prepared to pay for it. Some countries try to manage the float by buying and selling their own currencies to influence the market (a practice known inelegantly as a "dirty float"). Other countries peg the value of their money to that of a major currency or group of currencies so that, for example, as the French franc rises in value, their own currency rises too. Many European countries keep the value of their individual currencies within a predetermined range of other currencies in the group.

Surveillance

The change from the par value to the present open exchange system may seem to imply a loss of influence by the IMF. In fact, that is not the case, as the present approach requires the IMF to be even more deeply involved with members' economic policies that have bearing on money's exchange value. In changing over to the present system, the membership has asked the IMF to penetrate beyond the exchange value, which, after all, is the final result of a range of economic policies, to examine all aspects of the member's economy that cause the exchange value to be what it is and to evaluate the economy's performance candidly for the entire membership. In short, the present system demands greater transparency of members' policies and permits more scope for the IMF to monitor these policies. The IMF calls this activity "surveillance," or supervision, over members' exchange policies. Supervision is based on the conviction that strong and consistent domestic economic policies will lead to stable exchange rates and a growing and prosperous world economy.

Consultations

Through periodic consultations conducted in the member country, the IMF obtains information on whether the country is acting responsibly and openly in setting the conditions under which its currency is bought and sold by governments and private citizens of other countries, as well as information on the country's overall economic position. These consultations also provide an opportunity for the IMF to encourage the elimination of any restrictions the country might have imposed on the immediate transfer of its domestic money into foreign currencies. In the early years of the IMF, these periodic consultations were mandatory only for members that had placed restrictions on currency exchange, but since 1978 the IMF undertakes them with all members.

Consultations typically take place annually, but the Managing Director may initiate additional discussions if a member falls suddenly into serious economic difficulty or is believed to be following practices inimical to the interests of other members. Each year, a team of four or five IMF staff members travels to the

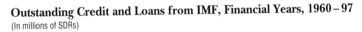

Outstanding Credit and Loans from IMF, Financial Years, 1960–97
(In millions of SDRs)

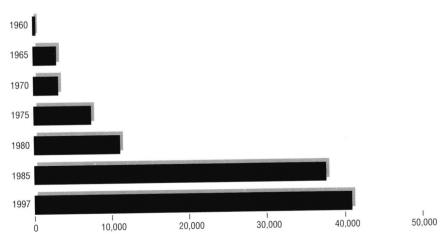

country's capital and spends about two weeks gathering information and holding discussions with government officials about the country's economic policies. The first phase of the consultation is devoted to collecting statistical data on exports and imports, wages, prices, employment, interest rates, how much money is in circulation, investments, tax revenues, budgetary expenditures, and other aspects of economic life that have a relation to the exchange value of money. The second phase consists of discussions with high-ranking government officials to find out how effective their economic policies have been during the previous year and what changes might be anticipated during the coming year, as well as to learn what progress the country has made in eliminating whatever restrictions it has placed on the exchange of its currency. When these meetings are over, the team returns to headquarters in Washington to prepare a detailed staff report for discussion by the Executive Board. The Executive Director representing the country of course takes part in this discussion with his colleagues, clarifying points about the country's economy and listening to the evaluation by other Executive Directors of the country's economic performance. A summary of the discussion, often containing suggestions about how to strengthen areas of economic weakness, is later transmitted to the member's government.

Besides these periodic discussions, the IMF also holds special consultations with those countries whose policies have a major influence on the world's economy. These special consultations review the world economic situation and evaluate anticipated economic developments. The IMF publishes the results of these reviews twice a year in its *World Economic Outlook*. This publication contains valuable information and projections for the world economy and, by highlighting various policy options, assists member countries in coordinating their own economic policies with anticipated policy developments in other member countries.

Financial Function

Although the IMF was founded primarily as a cooperative institution to oversee the international monetary system, it also sup-

> *"The IMF was founded primarily as a cooperative institution to oversee the international monetary system."*

ports that system by occasionally injecting into it sums of money, sometimes on a very large scale, through loans to its members. Indeed, the IMF is perhaps best known to the general public for pumping billions of dollars into the system during the debt crisis of the 1980s and for the vast amounts it committed to Mexico and to Russia during the 1990s. During 1983 and 1984, for example, the IMF lent some $28 billion to member countries having difficulty meeting their financial obligations to other members. In 1995, it extended to Mexico a credit of over $17 billion and to Russia more than $6.2 billion to help tide these countries over a difficult period of reform. The swift and well-publicized reaction of the IMF to this crisis might have misled observers into imagining that the IMF is first and foremost a lending institution. This is not the case, as the IMF remains primarily a supervisory institution for coordinating efforts to achieve greater cooperation in the formulation of economic policies. Nevertheless, its financial function is a significant activity.

Source of Finance

The quota subscriptions, or membership fees referred to earlier, constitute the largest source of money at the IMF's disposal. Quotas are now in theory worth about $210 billion, although in practice this sum is deceptively large. Because member countries pay 75 percent of their quotas in domestic money, and because most national currencies are rarely in demand outside the countries issuing them, approximately half of the money on the IMF's balance sheets cannot be used. Although there are occasional exceptions, only 20 or so currencies are borrowed from the IMF in the course of a typical year, and most potential borrowers from the IMF want only the major convertible currencies: the U.S. dollar, the Japanese yen, the deutsche mark, the pound sterling, and the French franc.

15

Principal Users of IMF Financing, 1947–97

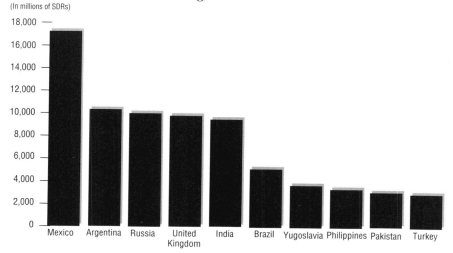

(In millions of SDRs)

As each member has a right to borrow from the IMF several times the amount it has paid in as a quota subscription, quotas might not provide enough cash to meet the borrowing needs of members in a period of great stress in the world economy. To deal with this eventuality, the IMF has had since 1962 a line of credit, now worth about $24 billion, with a number of governments and banks throughout the world. This line of credit, called the General Arrangements to Borrow, is renewed every five years. The IMF pays interest on whatever it borrows under these arrangements and undertakes to repay the loan in five years. These arrangements have been strengthened by a decision on the New Arrangements to Borrow, which when it enters into force will total $40–45 billion.

In addition to these arrangements, the IMF also borrows money from member governments or their monetary authorities for specific programs of benefit to its members. Over the past decade, using its good credit rating, the IMF has borrowed to provide needy members with more money for longer periods and under more favorable terms than they could obtain on their own. Borrowing these large amounts has to a certain extent changed the nature of the IMF, making it more like a bank, which is essentially an institution in the business of borrowing from one group and lending to another.

Financial Assistance

The IMF lends money only to member countries with payments problems, that is, to countries that do not take in enough foreign currency to pay for what they buy from other countries. The money a country takes in comes from what it earns from exports, from providing services (such as banking and insurance), and from what tourists spend there. Money also comes from overseas investment and, in the case of poorer countries, in the form of aid from better-off countries. Countries, like people, however, can spend more than they take in, making up the difference for a time by borrowing until their credit is exhausted, as eventually it will be. When this happens, the country must face a number of unpleasant realities, not the least of which are commonly a loss in the buying power of its currency and a forced reduction in its imports from other countries. A country in that situation can turn for assistance to the IMF, which will for a time supply it with sufficient foreign exchange to allow it to put right what has gone wrong in its economic life, with a view to stabilizing its currency and strengthening its trade.

A member country with a payments problem can immediately withdraw from the IMF the 25 percent of its quota that it paid in gold or a convertible currency. If the 25 percent of quota is insufficient for its needs, a member in greater difficulty may request more money from the IMF and can over a period of years borrow cumulatively three times what it paid in as a quota subscription.

In lending to a member more than the initial 25 percent of quota, the IMF is guided by two principles. First, the pool of currencies at the IMF's disposal exists for the benefit of the entire membership. Each member borrowing another's currency from the pool is therefore expected to return it as soon as its payments problem has been solved. In this way, the funds can revolve through the membership and are available whenever the need arises. Second, before the IMF releases any money from the pool, the member must demonstrate how it intends to solve its payments problem so that it can repay the IMF within its normal repayment period of three to five years (which in certain cases can be extended up to ten years). The logic behind these requirements is simple. A country with a payments problem is spending more than it is taking in. Unless economic reform takes place, it will continue to spend more than it takes in. Since the IMF has an obligation to the whole membership to preserve the financial integrity of its transactions, it lends only on condition that the member use the borrowed money effectively. The borrowing country therefore undertakes to initiate a series of reforms that will eradicate the source of the payments difficulty and prepare the ground for economic growth. Along with its request for a loan, the potential borrower presents to the IMF a plan of reform, typically undertaking to lower the value of its money in terms of other currencies (if its money has been overvalued), encourage exports, and reduce government expenditure. The specifics of the program are selected by the member, and hence the program of reform is the member's, not the IMF's. The IMF's only concern is that the policy changes are sufficient to overcome the member's payments problem and do not cause avoidable harm to other members. Depending on the seriousness of the payments problem and the amount the member wishes to borrow, the Executive Directors, representing the entire membership, judge whether the reform measures are in fact sufficient and whether the IMF can reasonably expect payment.

If the Executive Directors are satisfied that the reforms will solve the problem, the loan is disbursed in installments (usually over one to three years) tied to the member's progress in putting the reforms into effect. If all goes well, the loan will be repaid on time, and the member, with necessary reforms now in place, will come out of the experience economically stronger.

"The IMF lends to member countries with payments problems under a variety of mechanisms that differ according to the specific problems."

The IMF lends to member countries with payments problems under a variety of mechanisms that differ according to the specific problems they address. Two frequently used mechanisms are stand-by arrangements and extended arrangements. These provide a line of credit to a member having trouble in staying current in its foreign obligations to support a program of one to two years (in the case of stand-by arrangements) or three to four years (in the case of extended arrangements) to allow it time to reorganize its finances, restructure its economy, and take measures to restore growth. During the period of the program, the member can borrow from the IMF in installments up to the maximum value of the credit to make its foreign payment, on condition that it stays with its program of policy adjustments.

Over the past 25 years, the IMF has also lent to its members through a mechanism designed to address a temporary decline in the member's export earnings for reasons substantially beyond the member's control. Let us say that frost destroys most of the coffee beans that a member exports in order to earn the foreign exchange (U.S. dollars, for example) that goes to pay for the member's day-to-day financial obligations to other members. The member then applies to the IMF for a loan—known as compensatory and contingency financing—related to its loss of export revenue, that will supply it with the necessary dollars to stay current in its obligations until the next coffee harvest is exported and the normal flow of revenues resumes.

Another mechanism makes money available at low interest rates to poor nations while they radically restructure their economies to rid themselves of long-standing inefficiencies. A novel feature of this method of lending—known as structural adjustment lending—requires close coordination with the World Bank, the IMF's sister institution that works exclusively for the economic development of the world's poorer nations, in putting in place reforms that will eradicate the source of the payments difficulty and prepare the ground for economic growth. This mechanism is funded by voluntary contributions from member countries that, in a spirit of cooperation, forgo the market rate of interest they could otherwise have obtained on those funds. The IMF's better-off members have made available nearly $20 billion to finance this mechanism.

Charges

If a member borrows money from the IMF, it pays various charges to cover the IMF's operational expenses and to recompense the member whose currency it is borrowing. Presently the borrower pays in service charges and commitment fees about 1/2 of 1 percent of the amount borrowed and in interest charges about 4 percent (except for the structural adjustment mechanism described above, for which interest charges are much less). An IMF member earns interest on its quota contributions only if other members borrow its currency from the pool. How much the member earns varies but lately has been slightly less than 4 percent of the amount of its currency that other members have borrowed from the IMF. Both the interest charges a borrower pays to the IMF and the recompense a creditor receives from the IMF are slightly below market rates in keeping with the cooperative spirit of the institution.

SDRs

By supplying convertible money to a member country through these various means, the IMF helps stabilize the exchange value of the member's currency. The IMF is also able to create a special type of money to add to the reserve assets that most countries keep on hand as a cushion against any payments that might have to be settled in foreign exchange. As a rule of thumb, most countries find it prudent to keep on hand enough reserves to cover a few months' worth of payments. During the 1960s it appeared that the world economy might be slowed down because reserves were inadequate to back the robust economic expansion the world was then experiencing. The principal reserves during that era were gold and U.S. dollars, and there was a problem with the supply of each. The supply of gold was limited by the difficulty of finding and raising it from the ground. New supplies of gold could not keep pace with the rapid expansion of the world economy. The supply of dollars to be kept on reserve by other nations depended on the willingness of the United States to spend and invest abroad more money than it took in. Since the United States could not be counted on to continue to do so indefinitely, a long-range shortage of reserves was possible. In response to this possibility, its member governments empowered the IMF to issue the asset called the SDR (special drawing right), which members add to the holdings of foreign currencies and gold they keep in their central banks. An artificial value, based on the average worth of the world's five major currencies, is assigned to the SDR. Today there are 21.4 billion SDRs in existence, worth nearly $29 billion, accounting for about 2 percent of all reserves.

Valuation of the SDR

(In percent)

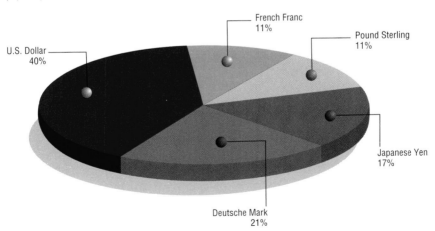

French Franc
11%

Pound Sterling
11%

U.S. Dollar
40%

Japanese Yen
17%

Deutsche Mark
21%

"Access to each member's fiscal, monetary, and external debt data has made the IMF a unique conduit of such information to the entire membership."

Services

Besides supervising the international monetary system and providing financial support to member countries, the IMF assists its membership by running an educational institute in Washington, by making technical assistance available in member countries in certain specialized areas of its competence, and by issuing a wide variety of publications relating to international monetary matters.

Since its founding at headquarters in Washington in 1964, the IMF Institute has offered courses and seminars to over 10,000 officials from virtually all member countries whose work is closely related to the work of the IMF. Most participants are employees of finance ministries, central banks, and other official financial agencies. The Institute has been highly successful over the years in acquainting its participants with how the monetary system works and what part the IMF plays in its operation. Training at the Institute has also helped to standardize throughout the world the methods of gathering and presenting balance of payments, monetary, and financial statistics to the benefit of the entire membership. In addition, IMF courses and seminars are offered at the Joint Vienna Institute operated by the IMF and other international organizations.

Because they sometimes lack personnel trained in highly technical areas of public finance and central banking, many countries turn to the IMF for assistance in solving problems in these areas or in providing an expert to work with government financial agencies until sufficient domestic expertise is developed. Such calls for assistance were especially frequent during the 1960s and 1970s when scores of newly independent nations were suddenly faced with setting up central banks, issuing new currencies, devising tax systems, and organizing the other financial and monetary systems of a modern sovereign state. The IMF responded by sending out experts from its own staff or experienced consultants to impart the required knowledge and training. During the 1990s, the decision of the countries of Eastern Europe, the Baltic countries, Russia, and the other countries of the former Soviet Union to move from central planning to a market-based economy and to enter the international monetary system has placed heavier demands than ever on the IMF's capacity to furnish technical assistance. Current requests are for specialized assistance in accounting, budget preparation, design of monetary instruments, social benefits and social security systems, development of money markets, bank regulation and supervision, statistics, research, law, tax policy, and management.

Access to each member's fiscal, monetary, and external debt data has made the IMF a unique conduit of such information to the entire membership. The IMF regards sharing statistical data as indispensable to the cooperative character of the institution. Almost since its inception, therefore, it has issued monthly and annual statistical publications, such as *International Financial Statistics,* that not only keep member countries informed of the financial position of their fellow members but also constitute an unrivaled source of statistical information for banks, research institutes, universities, and the media.

In a significant move toward developing standards to guide countries in disseminating economic and financial statistics to the public, the IMF in 1996 opened an electronic bulletin board on the Internet's World Wide Web. This bulletin board is designed to identify countries that have adhered to the standards and inform users where they may obtain the relevant data. The publication of financial data helps to make members' economic policies more transparent. It reinforces a trend of recent years, in which international organizations, commercial banks, academics, nongovernmental organizations, and the general public have increasingly looked to the IMF for information not readily available elsewhere.

In addition to its statistical publications—and the semiannual *World Economic Outlook*—the IMF puts out an *Annual Report* with comprehensive information on its work during the year under review, Occasional Papers on issues of finance, monetary policy, and developments of a national or regional nature, books and seminar volumes on the economic, institutional, and legal aspects of the international monetary system, a quarterly academic journal *(Staff Papers)* comprising the results of economic research by the Fund staff, Staff Country Reports on recent economic developments in member countries, the *IMF Survey* (a biweekly publication featuring articles on the IMF's work, and on national economies and international finance, the joint IMF-World Bank quarterly *Finance & Development,* and large numbers of working papers and other staff studies. In addition to the dissemination of printed material, the IMF's site on the World Wide Web makes freely available the texts of all of the IMF's complimentary publications, as well as the full texts of all staff working papers published since the beginning of 1997.

Recent Activities

The turbulent decade of the 1990s has presented the IMF with the most demanding challenges of its history. These new challenges have stimulated interest in ensuring that the IMF's mechanisms and operations fit the new world of integrated global markets for goods, services, and capital—known as globalization. In particular, the IMF acted to review further its surveillance operations, including in the areas of banking soundness, data dissemination, and the promotion of good governance. By responding flexibly to these changing needs and environment, the IMF continues to show itself an effective force in international monetary affairs.

Starting early in the decade, the IMF mounted a massive campaign to help the countries of Central Europe, the Baltic countries, Russia, and the other countries of the former Soviet Union in the difficult shift from centrally planned to market economies. Much of the effort focused on providing expertise in establishing those financial and economic structures (central banks, tax systems, currency convertibility, tariff regimes) essential for the functioning of a free-enterprise system. But financing was another important component of this support. In 1995, the IMF approved major funding for Russia and Ukraine, totaling about SDR 6.0 billion ($9.5 billion), followed in 1996 by additional funding for Russia totaling SDR 6.9 billion (more than $10 billion).

As part of the IMF's continuing efforts to promote economic growth and sound policies in the developing countries, it is cooperating with the World Bank in an initiative to help the most heavily indebted poor countries with a sound record of economic adjustment to surmount their debt problems.

In mid-decade, a financial crisis erupted in Mexico that showed the vulnerability of members to sudden shifts in market sentiments that lead to large and unpredictable capital outflows. Mexico moved quickly to enact a strong program of policy adjustments and the IMF also acted swiftly to help, approving, on February 1, 1995, the largest financing package ever agreed for a member country, a total of SDR 12.1 billion ($19 billion). This exceptional assistance was designed to give confidence to the international financial community and to stop contagion spreading from Mexico to other members.

In the wake of Mexico's financial crisis, the IMF has focused on preventing such crises in the future by strengthening surveillance of members' exchange rate policies and financial markets. It has taken steps to assess more candidly the potential risks attached to members' policies. It has sought more timely data, has exercised closer scrutiny over members' financial sectors and issues related to banking soundness, and has concentrated attention on countries where economic disturbances are likely to impinge broadly on the international community.

Also, the Interim Committee has endorsed the concept of an amendment to the IMF's charter that would make the promotion of capital account liberalization one of its purposes and give the IMF appropriate jurisdiction over capital movements.

The call on the IMF to provide financial support for Mexico, Russia, and Ukraine, as well as to other developing countries and economies in transition, has led to exceptionally heavy demands on resources. The IMF and its members are now considering extending emergency financing, increasing quotas, and issuing more SDRs to meet the needs of the membership in the prevailing world environment.

External Relations Pamphlets of the International Monetary Fund

Assisting Reform in Central and Eastern Europe, by John M. Starrels Revised 1992. In English, French, Russian, and Spanish

The Baltic States in Transition, by John M. Starrels. In English (1993), French (1994), Russian (1994), and Spanish (1994).

The Challenges of Globalization in an Independent World Economy, by Michel Camdessus. 1997. In English, French, and Spanish.

Dealing with the Unexpected: The IMF's Response to the Middle East Crisis, by David M. Cheney. 1991. In English, French, and Spanish.

Facing the Globalized World Economy: The IMF Experience, by Michel Camdessus. 1996. In English, French, and Spanish.

Funding the IMF: Why an Increase in Quotas? By Esha Ray. In English (revised 1992), French (1990), and Spanish (1990).

Helping the Poor: The IMF's New Facilities for Structural Adjustment, by Joslin Landell-Mills. In English (revised 1992), French (1988), and Spanish (1988).

The IMF and the World Bank: How Do they Differ? By David D. Driscoll. In English (revised 1994), French (revised 1994), German (1988), Russian (1992), and Spanish (revised 1992).

IMF Support for African Adjustment Programs: Questions and Answers, by F.L. Osunsade. In English (1993), French (1994), and Spanish (1994).

Promoting Development: The IMF's Contribution, by Bahram Nowzad. In English (reprinted 1991), French (1990), and Spanish (1990).

Promoting Economic Stability: The IMF's Compensatory and Contingency Financing Facility, by David M. Cheney and Luc D. Evaraert. Revised 1994. In English, French, and Spanish.

Ten Common Misconceptions About the IMF, by the External Relations Department, In English (revised 1993), French (1988), German (1988), Russian (1992), and Spanish (1988).

What Is the International Monetary Fund? By David D. Driscoll. In English (revised 1997), Chinese (1995), French (revised 1995), German (1988), Russian (1992), and Spanish (revised 1995).

Note: External Relations pamphlets are available free of charge. Please contact International Monetary Fund, Publication Services 700 19th Street, N.W., Washington, D.C. 20431, U.S.A.
Tel.: (202) 623-7430, Telefax: (202) 623-7201
E-mail: publications@imf.org
Internet: http://www.imf.org